The Kids' Music Collection

Songs compiled in this collection were very carefully selected for the "kid" in all of us. From our favorite nursery rhymes to the positive, uplifting "I Believe I Can Fly," all of these songs will bring hours of playing pleasure for Moms, Dads, big brothers and sisters, baby-sitters, day care teachers and even Grandmas and Grandpas. This book can be passed on from generation to generation because this music will always have a place in our childhood memories.

...Editor

WARNER BROS. PUBLICATIONS - THE GLOBAL LEADER IN PRINT
USA: 15800 NW 48th Avenue, Miami, FL 33014

WARNER/CHAPPELL MUSIC

CANADA: 85 SCARSDALE ROAD, SUITE 101
DON MILLS, ONTARIO, M3B 2R2
SCANDINAVIA: P.O. BOX 533, VENDEVAGEN 85 B
S-182 15, DANDERYD, SWEDEN
AUSTRALIA: P.O. BOX 353
3 TALAVERA ROAD, NORTH RYDE N.S.W. 2113

Carisch
NUOVA CARISCH

ITALY: VIA M.F. QUINTILIANO 40
20138 MILANO
SPAIN: MAGALLANES, 25
28015 MADRID

IMP
INTERNATIONAL MUSIC PUBLICATIONS LIMITED

ENGLAND: SOUTHEND ROAD,
WOODFORD GREEN, ESSEX IG8 8HN
FRANCE: 25 RUE DE HAUTEVILLE, 75010 PARIS
GERMANY: MARSTALLSTR. 8, D-80539 MUNCHEN
DENMARK: DANMUSIK, VOGNMAGERGADE 7
DK 1120 KOBENHAVNK

Editor/Project Manager: Carol Cuellar
Book Design: Joseph Klucar / Jorge Paredes

C000139196

CARTOON FAVORITES

MOTHER GOOSE RHYMES

PARTY & PLAY SONGS

PATRIOTIC FAVORITES

POPULAR FAVORITES

MOVIE & TV HITS

Cartoon Favorites

ANIMANIACS

Lyrics by
TOM RUEGGER

Music by
RICHARD STONE

Animaniacs - 3 - 1

From the Motion Picture "BATMAN" ™

THE BATMAN THEME

Music by
DANNY ELFMAN
Transcribed and Arranged by
TONY ESPOSITO

The Batman Theme - 5 - 1

The Batman Theme - 5 - 2

The Batman Theme - 5 - 4

JETSONS MAIN THEME
from THE JETSONS

Words and Music by WILLIAM HANNA,
JOSEPH BARBERA and HOYT CURTIN

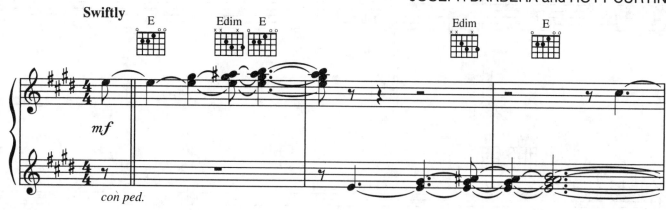

Meet George Jet - son!

Jetsons Main Theme - 3 - 1

(MEET) THE FLINTSTONES
from THE FLINTSTONES

Words and Music by
WILLIAM HANNA, JOSEPH BARBERA
and HOYT CURTIN

HUCKLEBERRY HOUND
from the Cartoon Television Series

Words and Music by WILLIAM HANNA,
JOSEPH BARBERA and HOYT CURTIN

I TAUT I TAW A PUDDY-TAT
(I Thought I Saw a Pussy-Cat)

Words and Music by
ALAN LIVINGSTON, BILLY MAY and WARREN FOSTER

Additional Lyrics

2. There is a great big bad old cat,
   Sylvester is his name,
   He only has one aim in life,
   And that is very plain.
   He dreams of catching Tweety Pie
   And eating him one day,
   But just as he gets close enough,
   Tweety gets away:

   Chorus:

3. Tweety sometimes takes a walk
   And goes outside his cage,
   But he gets back before the cat,
   And throws him in a rage.
   Sylvester'd love to eat that bird
   If he could just get near,
   But ev'rytime that he comes by,
   This is all he'll hear:

   Chorus:

4. And when he sings that little song,
   His mistress knows he's home,
   She grabs her broom and brings it down
   Upon Sylvester's dome.
   So there's no need of worrying,
   He lives just like a king,
   And puddy tats can't hurt that bird
   As long at he can sing:

   Chorus:

JOSIE AND THE PUSSYCATS
MAIN TITLE
(from the Cartoon Television Series)

Words and Music by
HOYT CURTIN, DENBY WILLIAMS
and JOSEPH ROLAND

Jo - sie and the Pus-sy - cats, _ long tails and ears for hats, _ gui - tars _ and sharps 'n' flats. _ Neat, sweet, a groov-y song, you're in - vit - ed, come a - long. __

TOP CAT
from the Cartoon Television Series

Words and Music by WILLIAM HANNA,
JOSEPH BARBERA and EVELYN TIMMENS

Top Cat,

the most ef-fec-tu-al Top ___ Cat, who's in-tel-lec-tu-al.

Close friends get to call him "T. C.," ___ pro-vid-ing it's

Top Cat - 3 - 1

LINUS AND LUCY

By
VINCE GUARALDI

Linus and Lucy - 4 - 1

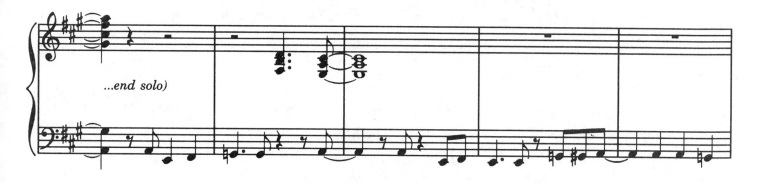

...end solo)

D. S. %% *al Coda*

A

Coda   N.C.   A

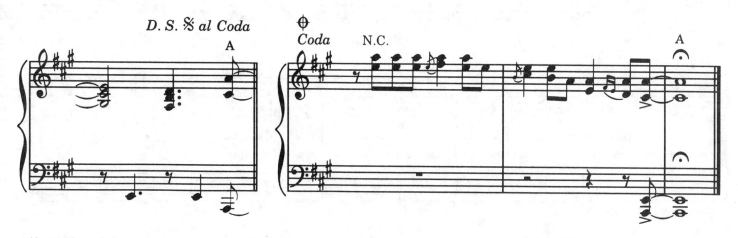

MERRILY WE ROLL ALONG

Words and Music by
EDDIE CANTOR, MURRAY MENCHER
and CHARLIE TOBIAS

Moderately

mf

C

Mer - ri - ly we roll a - long. My

D7

hon - ey and me,

G7

ver - i - ly there's no one half as

C

hap - py as we.

Am Ab+

Why we get a - long is ver - y eas - y to see.

C   Am   C   Am Ab+   G7

Though we're twice as poor as mice say what do we care?

Dm   Bb7

She and I won't buy un - less we pay for in cash.

Merrily We Roll Along - 2 - 1

THE MERRY-GO-ROUND BROKE DOWN

Words and Music by
CLIFF FRIEND and DAVE FRANKLIN

The Merry-Go-Round Broke Down - 2 - 1

MY LITTLE BUCKAROO

Words by
JACK SCHOLL

Music by
M.K. JEROME

My Little Buckaroo - 4 - 1

My Little Buckaroo - 4 - 2

SINGIN' IN THE BATHTUB

Words and Music by
HERB MAGIDSON, NED WASHINGTON
and MICHAEL H. CLEARY

day?   Par-don my e - la - tion, Ev-'ry-thing's just right,
splash!   Nev-er an - y troub-les Cross my bath-room path,

I get in - spir - a - tion, Ev-'ry Sat-ur-day night. I'm
Bath-ing in those bub - bles, I'm the knight of the bath. When

REFRAIN

Sing - in' in the bath - tub,   Hap - py once a - gain,
Sing - in' in the bath - tub,   Sit - tin' all a - lone,

p - f

Watch - in' all my troub - les go swing - in' down the
Tear - in' out a ton - sil, Just like a bar - i -

drain.
tone.

Sing-in' through the soap suds, ___
Nev- er take a show-er

Life is full o' hope, ___
It's an aw - ful pain, ___

You can sing with feel - ing, ___
Sing - in' in the show - er's, ___

While feel - ing for the soap.
Like sing - in' in the rain.

Oh, a
Oh, there's

ring a-round the bath - tub,
dirt to be a - bol - ished

Is - n't so nice to see, ___
But don't for-get one thing, ___

But a
While the

ring a-round the bath - tub, Is a rain - bow to
bod - y's washed and pol - ished, Sing, broth-er

me! Reach-in' for a tow - el Rea - dy for a rub,
sing. You can yo-del op'- ra Ev - en while you scrub

Ev - 'ry-bod - y's hap - py when sing - in' in the
Ev - 'ry-bod - y's hap - py when sing - in' in the

tub. tub.

THEME FROM "THE SIMPSONS"

Music by
DANNY ELFMAN

Moderately fast (♩ = 171)

Theme from "The Simpsons" - 4 - 2

a tempo

THEME FROM INSPECTOR GADGET
(Animated Cartoon Series)

Words and Music by
HAIM SABAN and SHUKI LEVY

Theme from Inspector Gadget - 2 - 1

TINY TOON ADVENTURES
Theme Song

Lyrics by
WAYNE KAATZ, TOM RUEGGER
and BRUCE BROUGHTON

Music by
BRUCE BROUGHTON

Tiny Toon Adventures - 2 - 1

WAKKO'S AMERICA

Lyrics by
RANDY ROGEL

TRADITIONAL

Moderate country two-beat

Ba - ton

A

Rouge, Lou - is - i - an - a, In - di - an - apo - lis, In - di - an - a, and Co - lum - bus is the cap - i - tal of

O - hi - o; there's Mont - gom - er - y, Al - a - bam - a, south of Hel - e - na, Mon - ta - na, then there's

58

just a quick jaunt, to Mont - pe - li - er which is up in Ver - mont,
wai - i's a joy, Jack - son, Mis - sis - sip - pi and Spring-field, Il - li - nois,

Hart-ford's in Con-nect - i - cut, so pret - ty in the fall, and Kan - sas has To - pe - ka, Min - ne -
South Ca - ro - li - na with Co - lum - bia down the way, and An - nap - o - lis in Ma - ry - land on

so - ta has St. Paul.
Ches - a - peake Bay.

(spoken) (They have wonderful clam chowder.)

Chey -

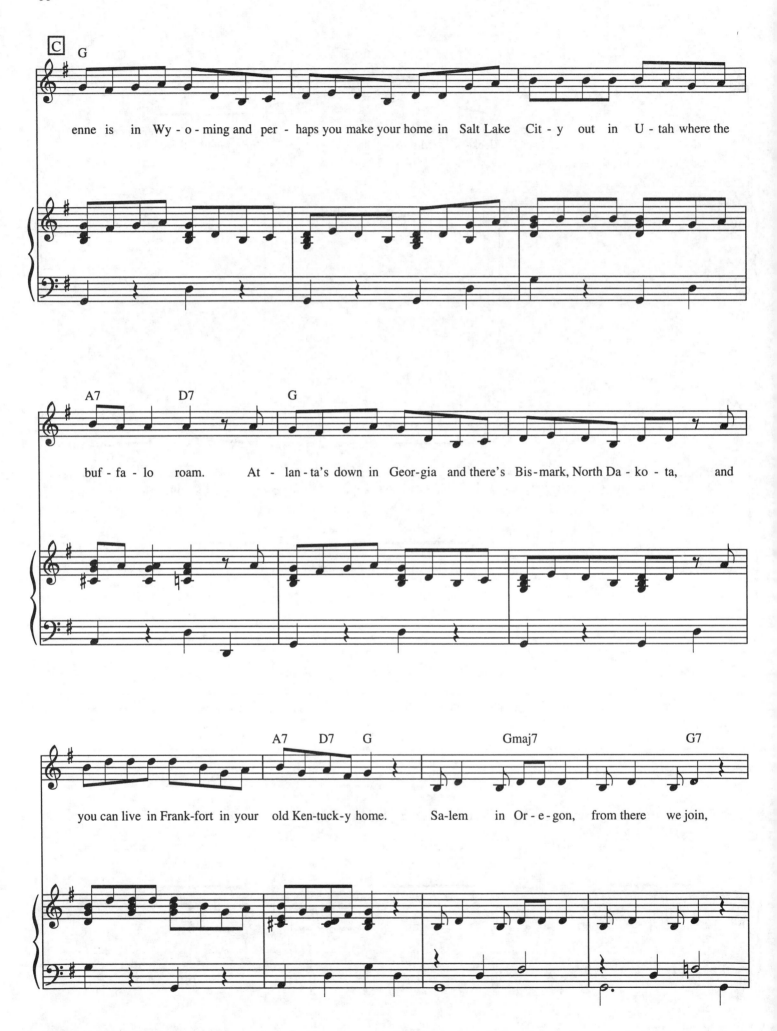

SCOOBY DOO MAIN TITLE
from the Cartoon Television Series

Words and Music by
WILLIAM HANNA, JOSEPH BARBERA
and HOYT CURTAIN

Scooby Doo Main Title - 2 - 1

Theme from "THE BUGS BUNNY SHOW"

THIS IS IT!

Words and Music by
MACK DAVID and JERRY LIVINGSTON

Mother Goose Rhymes

HEY, DIDDLE DIDDLE

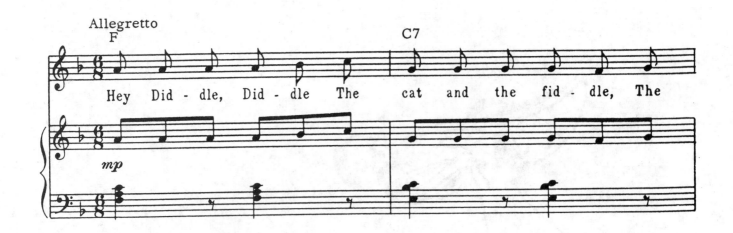

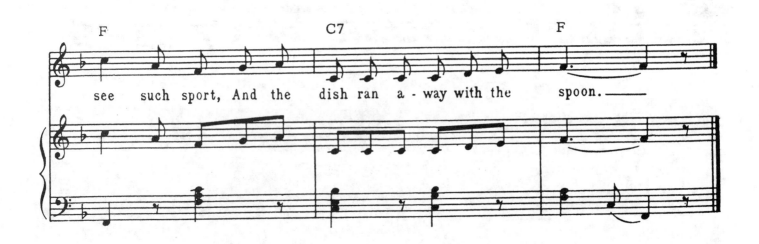

JACK AND JILL

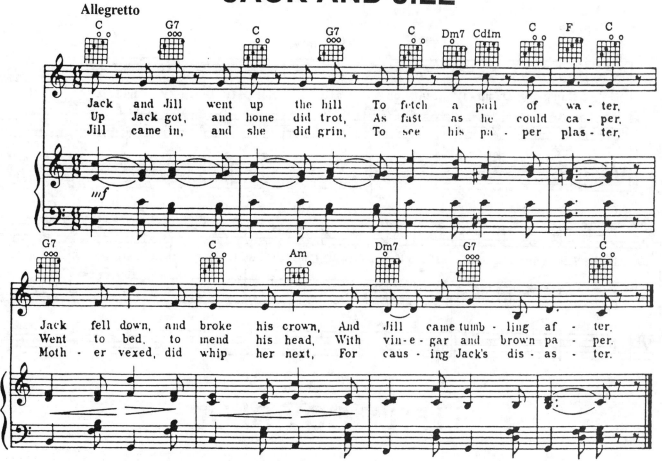

Allegretto

Jack and Jill went up the hill, To fetch a pail of wa-ter,
Up Jack got, and home did trot, As fast as he could ca-per,
Jill came in, and she did grin, To see his pa-per plas-ter,

Jack fell down, and broke his crown, And Jill came tumb-ling af-ter.
Went to bed, to mend his head, With vin-e-gar and brown pa-per.
Moth-er vexed, did whip her next, For caus-ing Jack's dis-as-ter.

HUMPTY DUMPTY

LITTLE BOY BLUE

PETER, PETER, PUMPKIN EATER

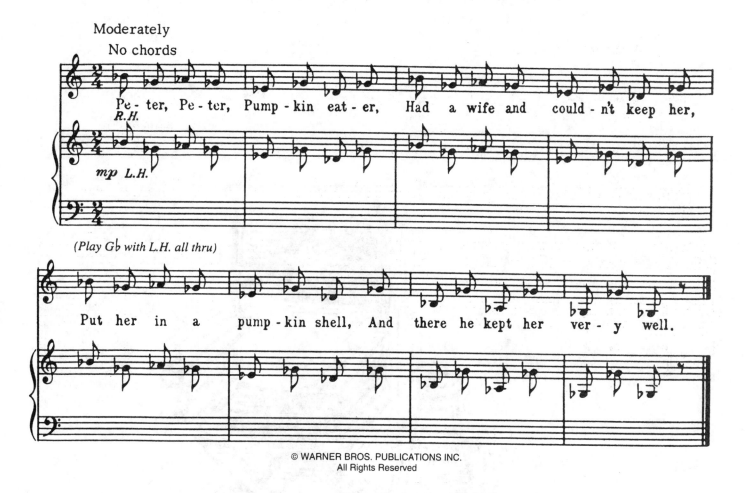

BAA! BAA! BLACK SHEEP

Movie & TV Hits

Theme from the Warner Bros. Animated TV Series "FREE WILLY"

FREE WILLY

Words and Music by
MICHAEL KAMEN

Free Willy - 3 - 1

ANNIE

Lyrics by
MARTIN CHARNIN

Music by
CHARLES STROUSE

Moderato

Lyrics under the staves:

An - nie,__ An - nie,__ An - nie,__ Ev - 'ry - thing's hum - ming now.
An - nie,__ An - nie,__ An - nie,__ Look what you've done__ for us.

An - nie,__ An - nie,__ An - nie,__ Good times are com - ing now,
An - nie,__ An - nie,__ An - nie,__ Turned on the fun__ for us.

Since she came our way It's Christ - mas, Christ - mas
All our hope was gone, And then you put sweet

Annie - 2 - 1

ev - 'ry day. We dis - miss bad times,__ sad times,__
dreams up - on the men - u. An - nie,__ An - nie,__

Now they're all yes - ter - day's news, since An - nie kicked out the
You filled our life__ with a song! We're glad you hap - pened a -

1. blues!_____

2. long!_____

Theme Song from the Mirisch-G&E Production, "THE PINK PANTHER," a United Artists Release

THE PINK PANTHER

Music by
HENRY MANCINI

The Pink Panther - 2 - 1

BEIN' GREEN

Words and Music by
JOE RAPOSO

84

From the Lucasfilm Ltd. Production - A Twentieth Century Fox Release "STAR WARS"

STAR WARS
(Main Theme)

Music by
JOHN WILLIAMS

Star Wars - 2 - 1

From the Motion Picture "SUPERMAN"

CAN YOU READ MY MIND?

Words by
LESLIE BRICUSSE

Music by
JOHN WILLIAMS

Can You Read My Mind? - 3 - 1

I BELIEVE I CAN FLY

Words and Music by
R. KELLY

used to think_that I___could not___ go on, and life was noth-ing but___ an aw-ful
I was on___ the verge_ of break-ing down. Some-times si - lence_ can seem_ so

IF I ONLY HAD A BRAIN

Lyrics by
E.Y. HARBURG

Music by
HAROLD ARLEN

If I Only Had a Brain - 3 - 1

Featured in the M-G-M Picture "THE WIZARD OF OZ"

WE'RE OFF TO SEE THE WIZARD
(The Wonderful Wizard of Oz)

Lyric by
E.Y. HARBURG

Music by
HAROLD ARLEN

We're Off to See the Wizard - 3 - 1

98

Chorus, Marcia Moderato

I'LL BE THERE FOR YOU

(Theme from "Friends")

Words by
DAVID CRANE, MARTA KAUFFMAN,
ALLEE WILLIS, PHIL SOLEM
and DANNY WILDE

Music by
MICHAEL SKLOFF

I'll Be There for You - 6 - 1

* Guitar fill reads 8va.

From the Lucasfilm Ltd. Production "RETURN OF THE JEDI" - A Twentieth Century-Fox Release.

LUKE AND LEIA

Music by
JOHN WILLIAMS

Luke and Leia - 2 - 1

From the Warner Bros. Motion Picture "SUPERMAN"

THEME FROM "SUPERMAN"

Music by
JOHN WILLIAMS

Theme from "Superman" - 4 - 1

Theme from "Superman" - 4 - 2

110

Theme from "Superman" - 4 - 3

From the Motion Picture "THE WIZARD OF OZ"

OVER THE RAINBOW

Words by
E.Y. HARBURG

Music by
HAROLD ARLEN

Over the Rainbow - 4 - 1

Theme from "GILLIGAN'S ISLAND" TV Series

THE BALLAD OF GILLIGAN'S ISLE

Words and Music by
SHERWOOD SCHWARTZ and
GEORGE WYLE

The Ballad of Gilligan's Isle - 2 - 1

From The United Artists Picture "HOLE IN THE HEAD"

HIGH HOPES

Words by
SAMMY CAHN

Music by
JAMES VAN HEUSEN

Lyrics:

1. Next time you're found____ with your chin on the ground,____ There's a
2. When trou-bles call____ and your back's to the wall,____ There's a

lot to be learned,____ So look a - round.____
lot to be learned,____ That wall could fall.____

Refrain

Just what makes that lit - tle ol' ant____ Think he'll move that
Once there was a sil - ly ol' ram,____ Thought he'd punch a

120

High Hopes - 4 - 3

Oops! There goes an - oth - er rub - ber tree plant. Oops! There goes an -
Oops! There goes a bil - lion kil - o - watt dam. Oops! There goes a
Oops! There goes an - oth - er prob - lem, ker - plop! Oops! There goes an -

oth - er rub - ber tree plant! Oops! There goes an - oth - er rub - ber tree
bil - lion kil - o - watt dam! Oops! There goes a bil - lion kil - o - watt
oth - er prob - lem, ker - plop! Oops! There goes an - oth - er prob - lem, ker -

1.2.

plant!
dam!

3.

plop! Ker - plop!

Featured in the M-G-M Picture "THE WIZARD OF OZ"

DING-DONG! THE WITCH IS DEAD

Lyrics by
E.Y. HARBURG

Music by
HAROLD ARLEN

Ding-Dong! The Witch Is Dead - 4 - 1

Chorus, Moderately

Ding - Dong, The Witch Is Dead! Which old witch? the wick - ed witch.

Ding - dong, the wick - ed witch is dead._____ Wake up, you

sleep - y head, rub your eyes, get out of bed. Wake up, the

wick - ed witch is dead!_____ She's gone where the gob - lins go be-

Main Title from "MIGHTY MORPHIN POWER RANGERS"

GO GO POWER RANGERS

Words and Music by
SHUKI LEVY and KUSSA MAHCHI

pow - er and a force that you've nev - er seen_ be - fore._
fate of the world is ly - ing in_ their hands._

They've
They

got
know

the ab - il - i - ty to morph and to
to on - ly use their

ev - en up_ the_ score._
weap-ons for_ de - fence._

132

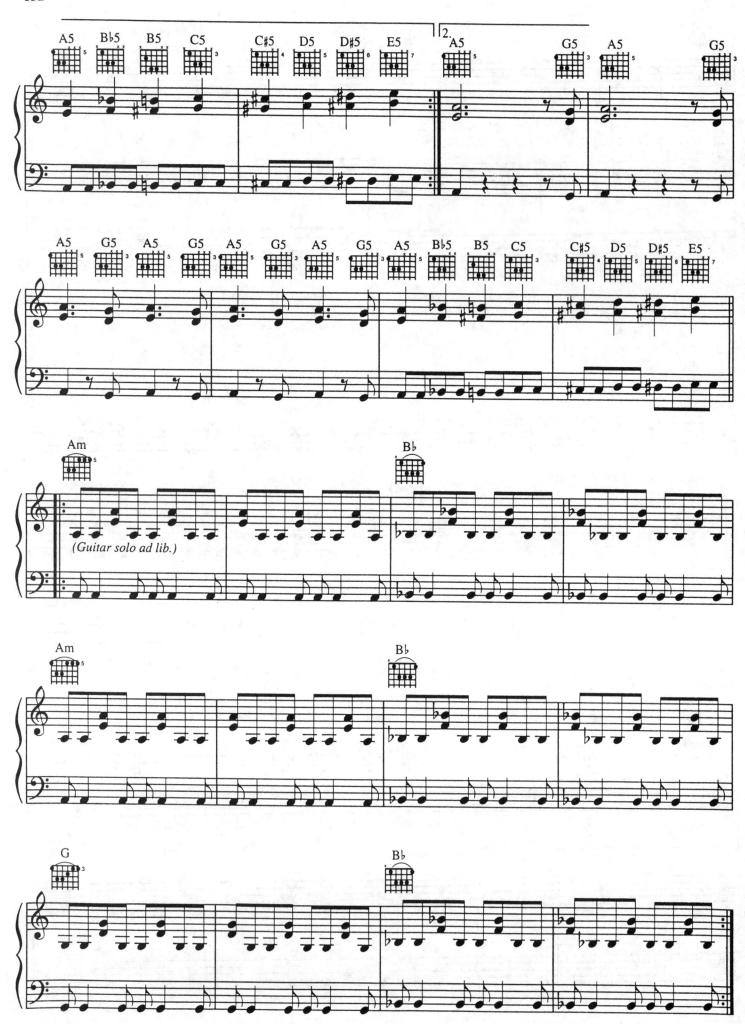

Party & Play Songs

"C" IS FOR COOKIE

Words and Music by
JOE RAPOSO

Now, what starts with the letter C?

Moderately slow ragtime ♩ = 120

Cookie starts with C. Let's think of other things that start with C. Ah, who cares about the other things!

1.2.4. C is for cook - ie, that's good e - nough for me! C is for cook - ie, that's
3. *(Spoken:) A round cookie with one bite out of it looks like a C.* *A round doughnut with one bite out*

good e - nough for me! C is for cook - ie, That's good e - nough for me! Oh,
of it looks like a C, but it is not as good as a cookie. *Oh, and the*

"C" Is for Cookie - 2 - 1

"A" YOU'RE ADORABLE
(The Alphabet Song)

Words and Music by
BUDDY KAYE, FRED WISE a
SIDNEY LIPPMAN

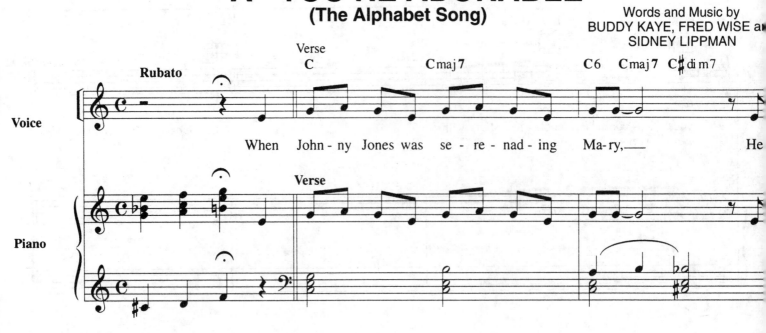

When John-ny Jones was se-re-nad-ing Ma-ry,—— He

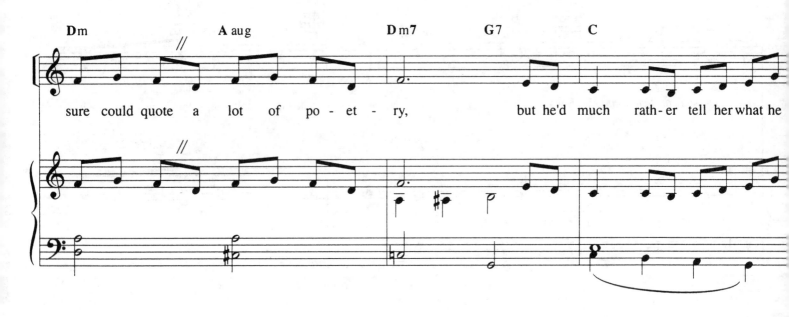

sure could quote a lot of po-et-ry, but he'd much rath-er tell her what he

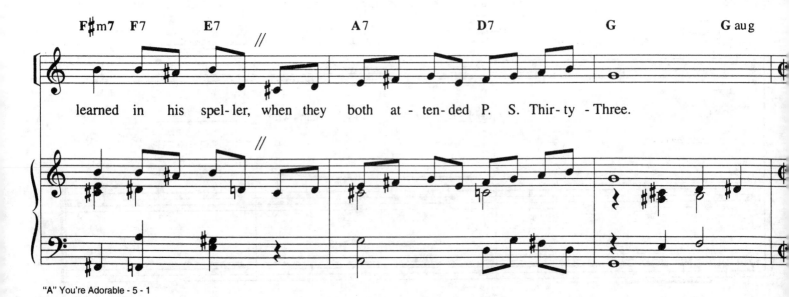

learned in his spel-ler, when they both at-ten-ded P. S. Thir-ty-Three.

"A" You're Adorable - 5 - 1

140

THE CHICKEN DANCE
(a.k.a. Dance Little Bird)

English Lyric
by PAUL PARNES

By TERRY RENDALL
and WERNER THOMAS

The Chicken Dance - 3 - 1

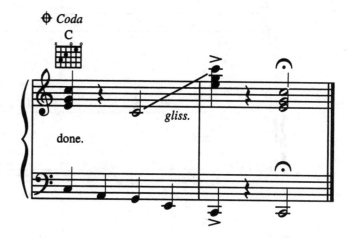

Verse 2:
Hey, you're in the swing.
You're cluckin' like a bird. (Pluck, pluck, pluck, pluck.)
You're flappin' your wings.
Don't you feel absurd. (No, no, no, no.)
It's a chicken dance,
Like a rooster and a hen. (Ya, ya, ya, ya.)
Flappy chicken dance;
Let's do it again. *(To Chorus 2:)*

Verse 3:
Now you're flappin' like a bird
And you're wigglin' too. (I like that move.)
You're without a care.
It's a dance for you. (Just made for you.)
Keep doin' what you do.
Don't you cop out now. (Don't cop out now.)
Gets better as you dance;
Catch your breath somehow. *(To Chorus 3:)*

Chorus 2:
Relax and let the music move you.
Let all your inhibitions go.
Just watch your partner whirl around you.
We're havin' fun now; I told you so.

Verse 4:
Now we're almost through,
Really flyin' high. (Bye, bye, bye, bye.)
All you chickens and birds,
Time to say goodbye. (To say goodbye.)
Goin' back to the nest,
But the flyin' was fun. (Oh, it was fun.)
Chicken dance was the best,
But the dance is done.

MACARENA

Words and Music by
ANTONIO ROMERO
and RAFAEL RUIZ

Da - le a tu cuer - po a-le - grí - a Ma-ca - re-na que tu cuer-po es pa' dar - le a-le-grí-a y co-sa bue-na.

Macarena - 6 - 1

Da - le a tu cuer - po a - le - grí - a Ma - ca - re - na, eh,_____ Ma - ca - re - na.

Verso 3:
Macarena sueña con el Corte inglés
Y se compra los modelos mas modernos.
Le gustaría vivir en Nueva York
Y ligar un novio nuevo.

Puente 2:
Macarena sueña con el Corte inglés
Y se compra los modelos mas modernos.
Le gustaría vivir en Nueva York
Y ligar un novio nuevo.
(Al Coro:)

Verso 4:
Macarena tiene un novio que se llama,
Que se llama de apellido Vitorino.
Y en la jura de bandera del muchacho
Se la dió con dos amigos.

Puente 3:
Macarena tiene un novio que se llama,
Que se llama de apellido Vitorino.
Y en la jura de bandera del muchacho
Se la dió con dos amigos.
(Al Coro:)

MAIRZY DOATS

Words and Music by
JERRY LIVINGSTON,
MILTON DRAKE and AL HOFFMAN

HAPPY BIRTHDAY TO YOU

Words and Music by
MILDRED J. HILL and PATTY S. HILL

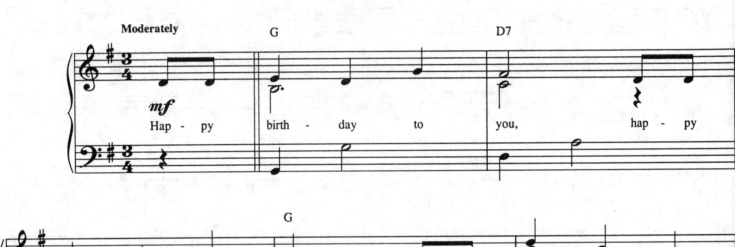

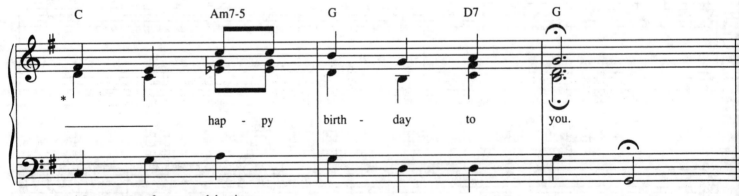

* Insert name of person celebrating.

Patriotic Favorites

ANCHORS AWEIGH

Words and Music by
Captain ALFRED H. MILES U.S.N.(Ret.), CHARLES A. ZIMMERMAN
and GEORGE D. LOTTMAN

Anchors Aweigh - 2 - 1

THE STAR-SPANGLED BANNER

Words by
FRANCIS SCOTT KEY

Music by
JOHN STAFFORD SMITH

AMERICA
(My Country 'Tis of Thee)

Words by
REV. SAMUEL F. SMITH

TRADITIONAL MELODY

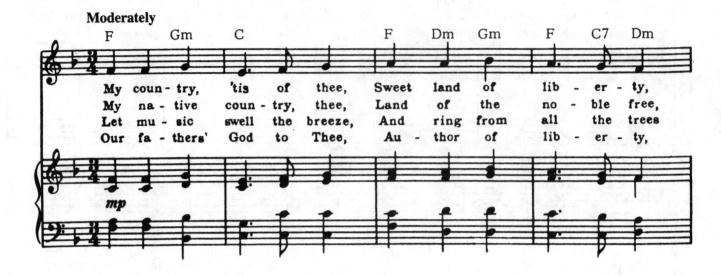

AMERICA THE BEAUTIFUL

Words by
KATHERINE LEE BATES

Music by
SAMUEL A. WARD

Popular Favorites

I'D LIKE TO TEACH THE WORLD TO SING
(In Perfect Harmony)

Words and Music by
B. BACKER, B. DAVIS,
R. COOK and R. GREENAWAY

I'd like to build the world a home and fur-nish it with love,

Grow ap-ple trees and hon-ey bees and snow-white tur-tle doves.

I'd like to teach the world to sing in per-fect har-mo-ny, I'd

I'd Like to Teach the World to Sing - 3 - 1

I'd Like to Teach the World to Sing - 3 - 3

DOES YOUR CHEWING GUM LOSE ITS FLAVOR ON THE BEDPOST OVER NIGHT?

(Does the Spearmint Lose Its Flavor on the Bedpost Overnight?)

Words and Music by
BILLY ROSE, MARTY BLOOM and ERNEST BREVER

Does Your Chewing Gum Lose Its Flavor on the Bedpost Over Night? - 2 - 1

THE SONG THAT DOESN'T END

Music and Lyrics by
NORMAN MARTIN
Arranged by MARTY GOLD

Medium bright

v.1

This is the

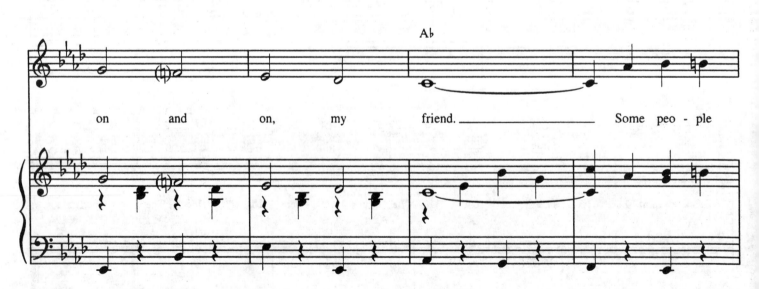

song that does-n't end, _____ yes, it goes

on and on, my friend. _____ Some peo-ple

The Song That Doesn't End - 4 - 1

170

Eb   Eb6   C7

singing it not know-ing what it was, and they'll con-tin-ue

Repeat to C *and fade*

F7

sing-ing it for-ev-er just be-cause, this is the

SING

Words and Music by
JOE RAPOSO

From the Motion Picture "DOCTOR DOLITTLE"

TALK TO THE ANIMALS

Words and Music by
LESLIE BRICUSSE

Talk to the Animals - 3 - 1

TAKE ME OUT TO THE BALL GAME

Words by
JACK NORWORTH

Music by
ALBERT VON TILZER

From the Broadway Musical "ANNIE"

TOMORROW

Lyrics by
MARTIN CHARNIN

Music by
CHARLES STROUSE

Moderately slow

The sun-'ll come out__ to-mor-row, bet your bot-tom dol-lar that to-

mor-row__ there'll be sun! Jus' think-ing a-bout__ to-mor-row

clears a-way the cob-webs and the sor-row__ till there's none. When I'm stuck__ with a

Tomorrow - 3 - 1

(small notes are optional harmony)